A very special thank you to Logan Burkett for his incredible editing skills and to all my friends and family who supported me.

Thank you and never stop pursuing your dreams!

Rachel Lassman

To Skylynn
Never stop learning!
12-17-22

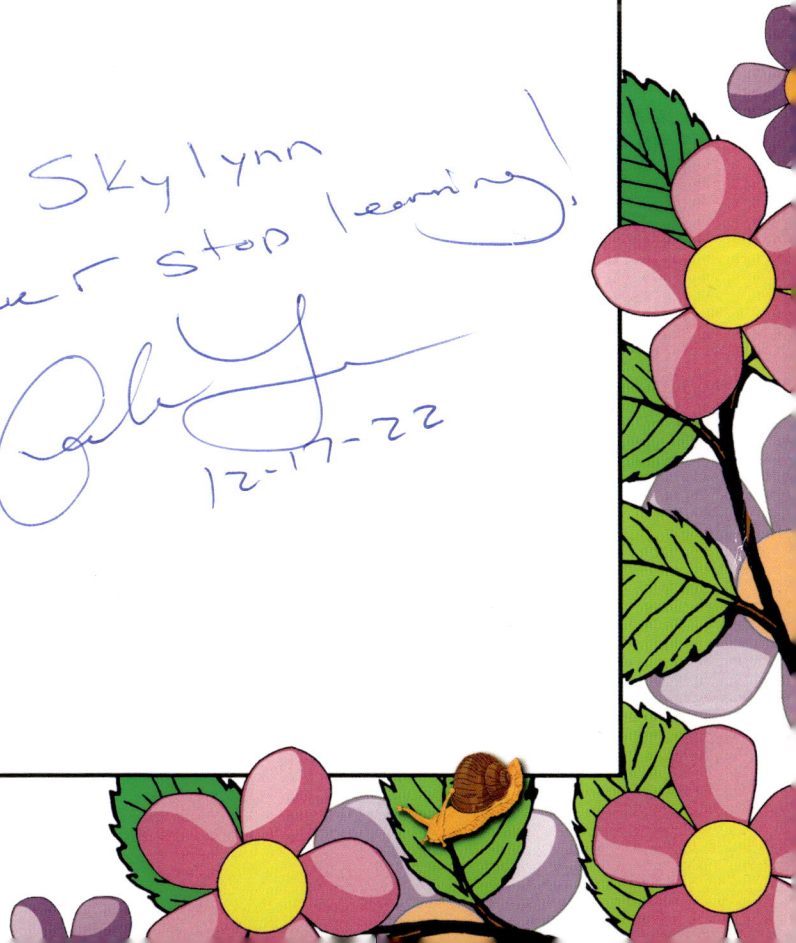

"Teacher!" yelled Billy.
"I don't know what I found.
There are so many trails
All over the ground!
They came out of the garden,
By the side of the school,
The one with the flowers,
And look kind of like drool!"

Drool? thought his teacher.
Then the answer was clear.
"I am certain I know
What we're dealing with here!
Come outside with me, Billy.
To the garden we go,
And I'll show you a critter
That's incredibly slow."

"The critters that made these
Are the common land snails.
They produce a thick mucus
Which creates all these trails.
This mucus protects them
From sharp things in the dirt,
That could cut their soft skin
And leave them terribly hurt."

"There are two other ways
In which mucus is used.
So, make sure you listen
So you don't get confused.
Snail's skin must stay moist
Or they can't survive.
So, it coats their whole body
And helps keep them alive."

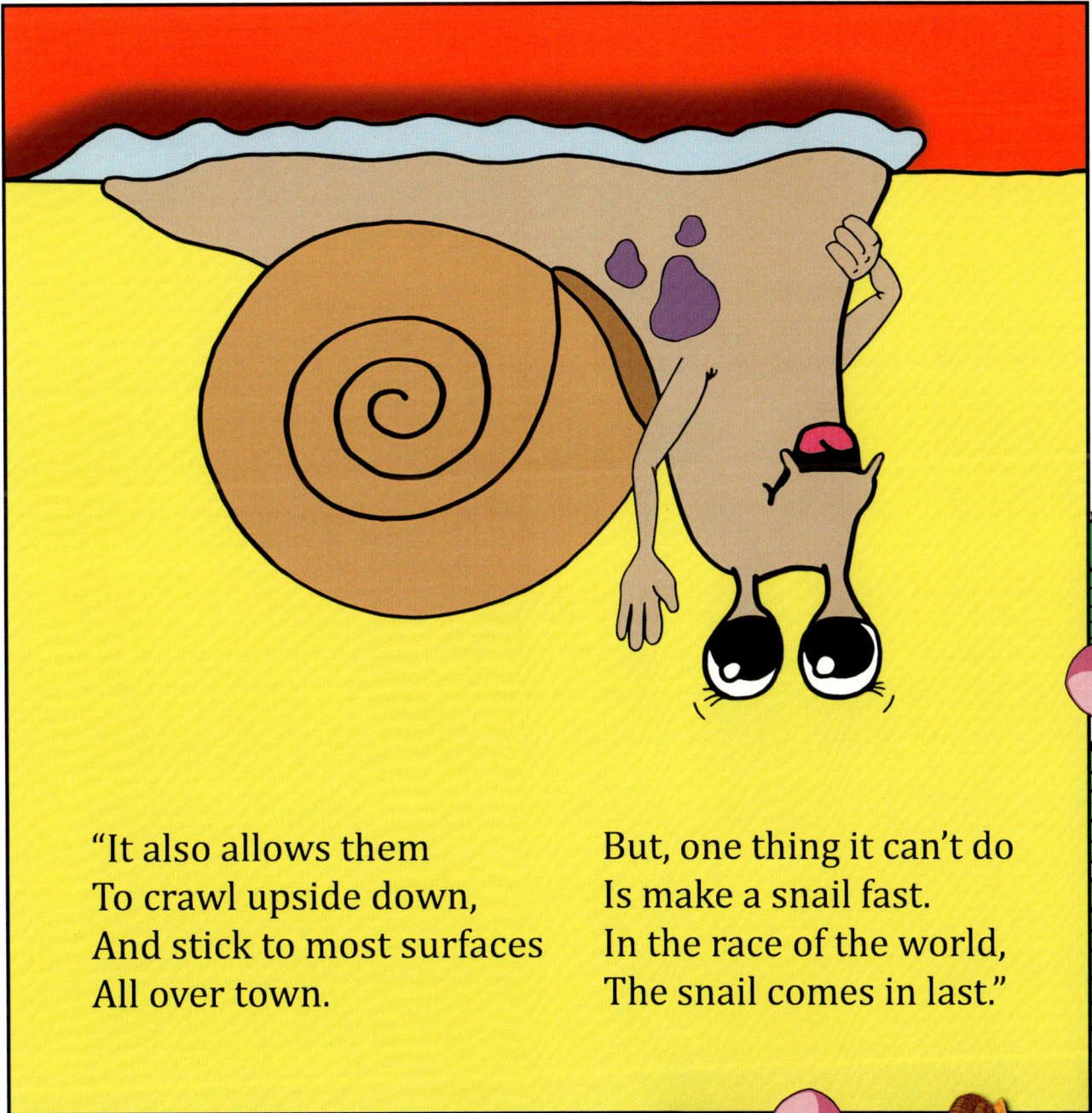

"It also allows them
To crawl upside down,
And stick to most surfaces
All over town.

But, one thing it can't do
Is make a snail fast.
In the race of the world,
The snail comes in last."

"Even at top speed,
The snail stands alone
As the slowest land animal
The world has known.

To understand the speed
Of their slow moving style,
They'd need over a day
To just crawl one mile!"

1 MILE RACE

TIME: 24hr

FINISH

"Over a day!" shouted Billy.
"That's incredibly slow.
Is it because of their shell?
I just have to know."
"Well, a shell gives protection
When a snail needs to hide.
They pull in their whole body
And fit nicely inside."

"Because of this shelter
Attached to their back,
Speed never evolved,
There was no need to go fast.
Although it looks heavy,
And hard to carry around,
It's not a shell's weight
That slows a snail down."

"It's because a snail's body
Has no bones at all.
They walk only with muscles
Which creates their slow crawl.

The main part of their body,
Which is under their shell,
Is called a snail's 'foot'
And moves them quite well."

I have no bones!

X-RAY

"But, it's not like the foot
That you and I know.
Their foot makes small ripples
When a snail needs to go.

You're not us!

"Wow," said young Billy.
"I never knew that before.
I can see the foot moving.
You must tell me more!"

"Snails are not insects.
They are not even bugs.
They're actually animals
And related to slugs.
But, they're different from animals
Like horses and cats.
They belong to the mollusks.
Let me tell you some facts."

"Some mollusks you know are
The octopus, squid, and clam.
They all have soft bodies.
Most don't live on the land.

Most live in the ocean,
And fresh water too,
Which means they have gills
That water goes through."

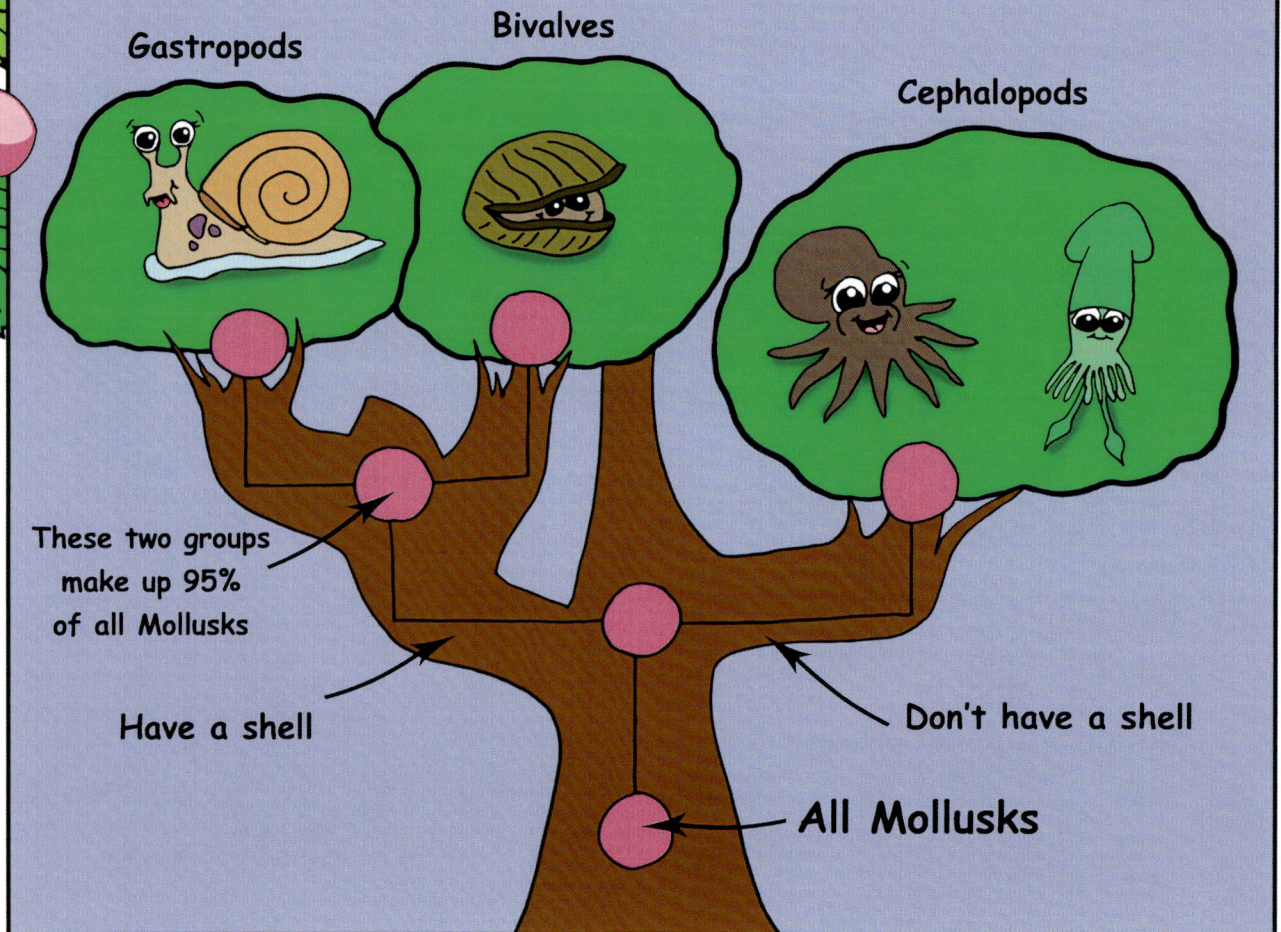

Gastropods

Bivalves

Cephalopods

These two groups
make up 95%
of all Mollusks

Have a shell

Don't have a shell

All Mollusks

"But, a few types of mollusks
Are unique from the rest.
They actually breathe air
And have lungs in their chest.
The land slug and land snail
Are two of these kinds,
And the only two mollusks
On land you will find."

"Both cannot breathe
Through their mouth or their nose.
So, there's a hole on their side
They can open and close.

Operculum
"Air Hole"

Except for the shell,
Which slugs tend to lack,
They're incredibly similar
From their front to their back."

Page 14

"Since a shell gives protection
From predators and drought,
A slug must be careful
To avoid drying out.
But, not having a shell
Lets a slug fit and squeeze
Into places snails can't
And can do it with ease."

"So, the features they have,
As you can see,
Have good points and bad
And make them unique.
But, there's much more to snails
We have yet to explore.
So, sit down beside me
And I'll tell you some more."

"According to fossils
Found deep in the ground,
They're one of the oldest
Known species around.

Although the exact date
Will never be clear,
They've survived for at least
500 million years!"

"Their life span's impressive.
I'm not sure you've been told.
But, the land snail can live
Up to fifteen years old.
But, getting that old
Can be a difficult feat,
As there are many small critters
That eat snails as a treat."

"Though most snails are small,
And not known for their size,
The Giant African Snail
Can sure take the prize.
They are known as the largest
Land snail that's been found,
Growing up to eight inches
And weighing nearly two pounds!"

2 LBS

.07 LBS

Weights 4 Life

"That's a really big snail!"
Said Billy with joy.
"Now, how do you know if
They're a girl or a boy?"
"That's a great question, Billy.
But, there's no way to know.
As it turns out that snails
Are actually both!"

"All snails lay eggs,
One hundred at a time.
They are tiny and white
And all covered in slime.
Snails are all born with
Their shells on their back.
But, they're fragile and thin
And can easily crack."

"They must eat the right foods,
Just like you and me,
To make sure they grow
To be strong and healthy.
Vegetables and plants
Are the foods that they eat,
Which quickly can make them
A pest to defeat."

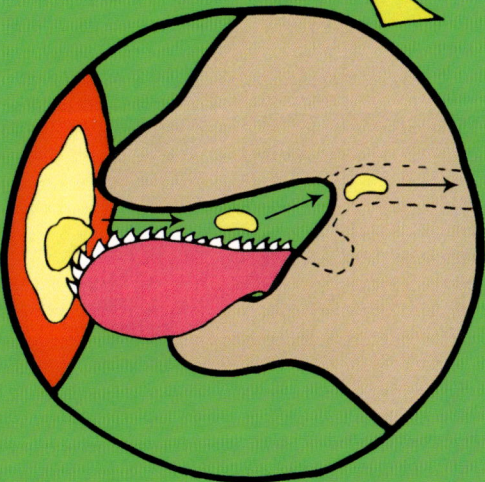

"But, their mouth is much different
From yours and from mine.
They eat with their tongue
When it's time to dine.
Their tongue's called a radula,
And it's covered with teeth.
It scrapes food in their mouth
Instead of chewing to eat."

"So, the next time you find
A snail in your yard,
If you stay nice and quiet
And listen real hard,
You can actually hear them
Scraping away
On whatever good food
They are eating that day."

"You may also notice
Things will move on their head.
These are called tentacles,
Known as feelers instead.
Both pairs of feelers
Can suck in or pull back,
When a snail feels in danger.
This is known as retract."

"A snail's life is simple.
There's not much they should know.
Just how to find food
And where they should go.
Since a snail has no ears,
They cannot hear a sound.
They must use other senses
When they move around."

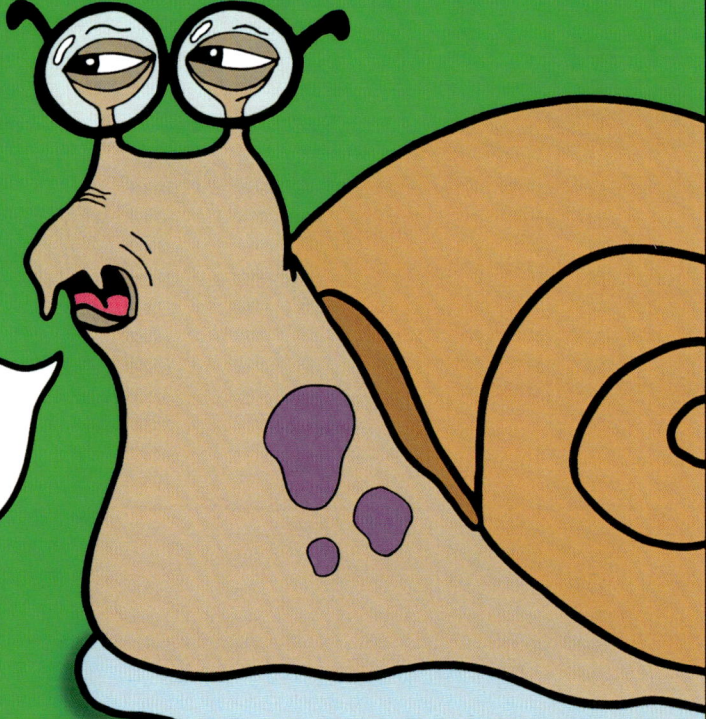

"The top feelers are for sight,
Though their vision's quite poor.
They see objects and shadows
Yet unknown how much more.
Their bottom two feelers,
Though smaller in size,
Are more important to snails
Then you may realize."

"These feelers help snails
In three different ways.
They not only can smell,
But can touch things and taste.
Now, there's just one more thing
Before we should go.
One final snail fact
That I think you should know."

"Like most other animals,
Snails have blood and a heart.
Though both of these things
Are much different from ours.
Our heart has four chambers,
While theirs just has two,
And though our blood is red,
A snail's blood is blue!"

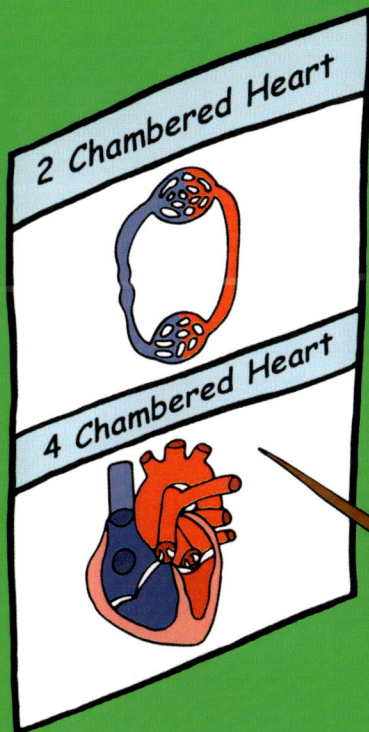

2 Chambered Heart

4 Chambered Heart

"That's amazing!" said Billy.
"I'm so happy I know
That there's much more to snails
Than them just being slow.
They have shells that protect them,
And no bones at all.
They make a thick mucus
That helps them to crawl."

"They walk on a foot,
And breathe with their lungs.
They have blue-colored blood,
And are related to slugs.
They're actually animals,
One of the oldest around,
And the largest land snail
Is nearly two pounds!"

"They can live fifteen years,
And can't hear at all.
So, use four special feelers
When they need to crawl.
Thank you," said Billy.
To his teacher with glee.
"There's so much to snails
That you just taught to me!"

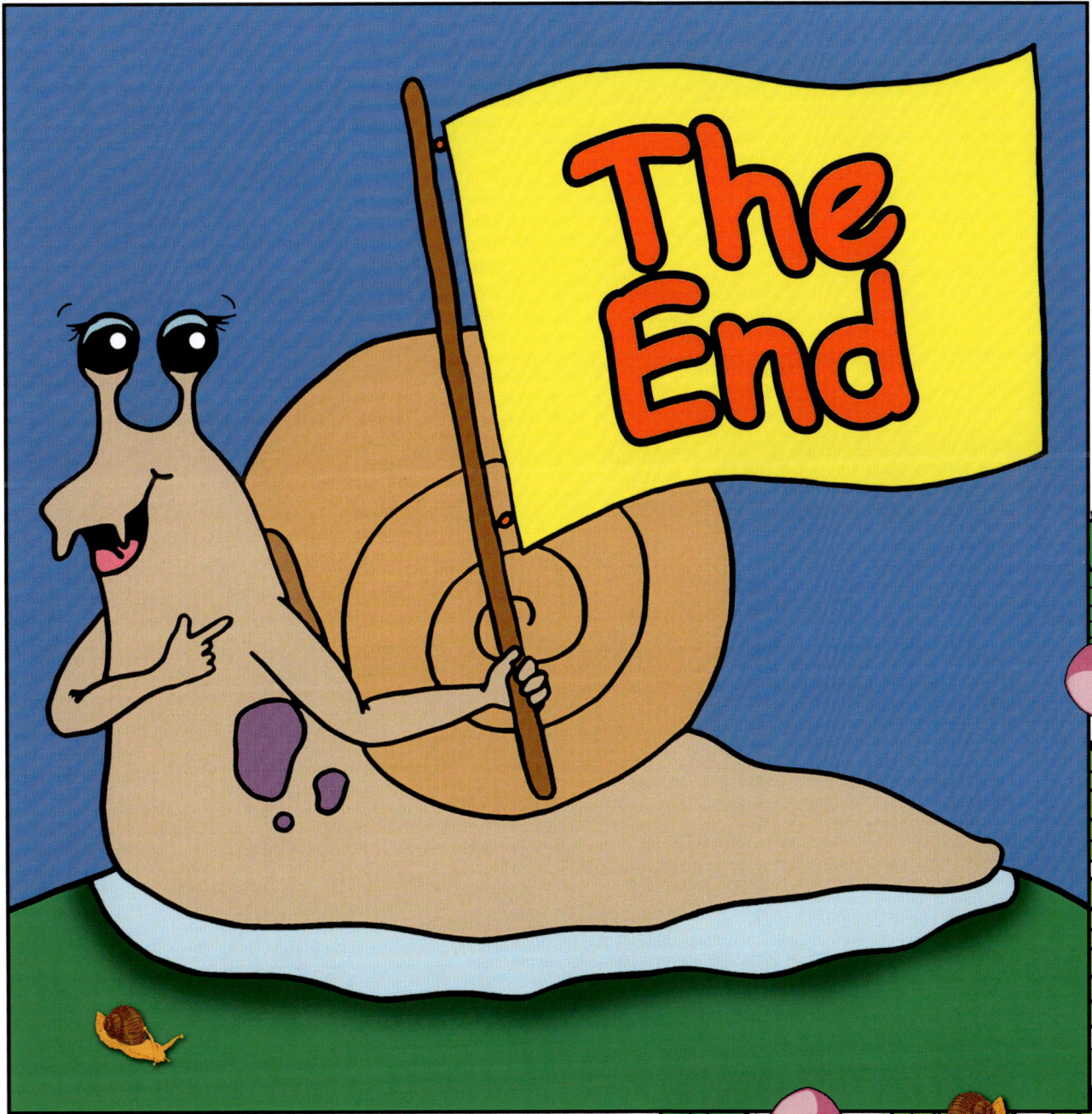

Favorite Snail Facts: